Coyote's Song

GAIL ANDERSON-DARGATZ

Coyote's Song

Grass Roots Press

First published in 2012 by Grass Roots Press

Grass Roots Press gratefully acknowledges the financial support for its publishing programs provided by the following agencies: the Government of Canada through the Canada Book Fund and the Government of Alberta through the Alberta Foundation for the Arts.

Alberta Foundation for the Arts

Grass Roots Press would also like to thank ABC Life Literacy Canada for their support. Good Reads® is used under licence from ABC Life Literacy Canada.

Library and Archives Canada Cataloguing in Publication

Anderson-Dargatz, Gail, 1963–
     Coyote's song / Gail Anderson-Dargatz.

(Good reads series)
ISBN 978-1-926583-83-9

     1. Readers for new literates. I. Title.
II. Series: Good reads series (Edmonton, Alta.)

PS8551.N3574C69 2012   428.6'2   C2012-902310-8

Printed and bound in Canada.

For my friends in the Shuswap

Chapter One

Coyote still walks this earth, stirring up trouble for us. I know that for a fact. He sure stirred up trouble for me.

Coyote is that trickster spirit my granny told me about. He was the most important of the animal spirits in my people's stories. My people are one of the many First Nations who live in British Columbia. My ancestors were here long before anyone came from Europe or anywhere else.

Granny said the Old One, the Great Spirit my people believed in, put Coyote on this earth to help make things right. Coyote gave my people salmon and taught us how to catch them, for example. But Coyote also loved to play tricks on people, just like he did on me.

One minute I was happy enough. I was married to a decent guy and had a wonderful daughter. I liked being a stay-at-home mom. The next minute, well, let's just say Coyote turned my life upside down.

I first saw Coyote at the big Roots and Blues Festival in the town of Salmon Arm. This festival attracts musicians and crowds from all over.

But I didn't know the animal I saw at the festival was the Coyote spirit. At first, I thought it was a dog. Then I thought it was an ordinary coyote. But I soon found out how wrong I was.

My daughter Rose and I stood in front of a festival stage. We listened to Fred Penner, who played his guitar and sang for the children. My daughter danced to his music with some of the other kids in the crowd.

Young Rose was already a performer, like me. She loved to dress up. She loved to dance and sing, just as I once had.

Rose would start kindergarten in a month, in September. The thought of my daughter starting school made me sad. I would be all alone at home during the day. I wasn't sure what I would do with my time. Sometimes I wasn't sure who I was anymore. I was "Mommy," I was Rob's wife, and I liked being both. But what about me, Sara?

My daughter looked like me. She had the same long, dark hair. She had my dark brown eyes. Her high cheekbones were the same as mine. She also had my long arms and legs, a dancer's body.

I took a photo of my daughter as she lifted her arms and danced to the music. Then I saw an animal trotting towards me through the crowd. It was a dog—no, it was a coyote. The other people at the music festival didn't seem to see it. The coyote sat in front of the stage and looked at me.

"Do you see that?" I asked my daughter. I pointed at the coyote. But Rose watched the singer on stage. I couldn't pull her attention away.

I saw coyotes all the time in the fields and on the golf course. I saw them in my backyard on the Native reserve where I live. I even saw them in town sometimes, trotting across lawns. But coyotes are wild animals; they run away from people. This one just sat in the middle of the crowd.

I snapped a picture of the coyote with my camera to show my daughter later. Then, through my camera lens, I saw my old friend Jim standing right beside the animal.

Jim and I were in a band years before, when I was in my twenties. The band played country music. Jim was the lead guitarist and singer. I was the backup singer. I hadn't seen Jim for many years.

In the view screen of my camera, Jim hadn't aged a day. His hair was black and shiny. His skin was brown and without wrinkles. He looked exactly the same as when I knew him nearly fifteen years before. How was that possible?

I took his picture and lowered my camera. I planned to wave at him. But he disappeared. I checked the photo on my camera screen. Jim wasn't in the picture I just took. Neither was the coyote.

But the coyote was still standing right there in front of me. Why hadn't the coyote shown up in my photo? Why hadn't Jim shown up in the picture? Were they both ghosts?

I knew then that something really strange was happening.

The coyote nodded its head as if to say, "Follow me." Then it trotted off.

Chapter Two

The coyote wove a path through the festival crowd. Its grey, brown, and yellow fur shone in the sun. Now, I saw that the coyote was a handsome animal. And it was bigger than any coyote I had seen before.

But no one except me seemed to see it. People walked by the coyote as if it wasn't there. I was surprised that people in the crowd didn't notice it. Then I lost sight of the animal.

I held out my hand to my daughter. "Come on, honey," I said. Rose wore a bright red dress. I had picked it out so I could see her easily in the crowd. Her black hair was pretty against the red.

"Where are we going, Mommy?" Rose asked me.

"I just saw an old friend," I said. "I want to see if I can find him." I didn't really believe Jim was a ghost. He had to be there somewhere.

"But Daddy was going to meet us here." Rob, my husband, had gone to another stage while we watched the children's show. He said he would return to Fred Penner's stage to meet us.

"We'll come right back," I told Rose.

We made our way through the crowd. But there were so many people. I looked and looked. Finally, I realized I didn't have a hope of finding Jim.

The music festival was spread over a huge field. Several bands played their music on different stages and under tents. The smell of hamburgers and fries floated through the air from the many food stands.

"I'm hungry," Rose said.

"All right," I said. "Let's go find Daddy. Then we'll grab some lunch."

My daughter and I turned to go back to the stage where the children's performer played. But I immediately bumped into Rob. He was following us, trying to catch up.

"Are you looking for me, Sara?" Rob grinned. He was sweating a little. The summer heat gave his handsome brown face a nice glow. He wore jeans and a T-shirt that showed off the muscles in his arms and shoulders.

"I thought I saw Jim in the crowd," I said. "I went to find him."

"Who?"

"Jim was the lead singer in that band I was in. We sang together in bars and clubs all over the province."

"You dated this guy?"

"No. We were just friends."

I did have a crush on Jim back then, though. Maybe I was even in love with him. But that was a long time ago.

"I take it that he didn't see you," Rob said.

"I'm not sure he would recognize me. He hasn't seen me for years."

Fred Penner started another song for the children. So we all went to watch the rest of the show. Rose danced in front of us, twirling in circles. Her red dress spread out around her as she whirled.

"Did you see that coyote running around?" I asked my husband.

"You saw a coyote? Here?" Rob laughed. "You probably just saw somebody's dog."

"No, it was a coyote," I said.

"Maybe someone has one for a pet," my husband suggested.

"Maybe," I said. But I wondered if the animal was even real. The coyote hadn't shown up in my photos. Could it have been the Coyote spirit from my grandmother's stories?

I pointed my camera to take a few more pictures of Rose. Through the camera lens I saw the coyote sitting in front of the stage again! My old friend Jim stood beside the coyote. But when I lowered my camera, Jim was gone. The coyote was still there, though.

I looked over the crowd, trying to see Jim. But he had disappeared. The coyote nodded its head, once again telling me to follow. Then it trotted off.

"Can you watch Rose for a minute?" I asked Rob.

"What's going on?"

I didn't try to explain. If I told my husband I was following the Coyote spirit, he would think I was crazy. But I knew this coyote was leading me to Jim. Still holding my camera, I pushed through the crowd to find my old friend.

Chapter Three

The coyote started to run. I ran after it, bumping into people as I went. Then the coyote was just gone! I stopped to look for it and found myself in front of another stage.

A band played country music there. I glanced up and saw my old friend Jim on stage. The coyote had led me right to him. That was so strange, I laughed out loud.

Jim played his guitar as a drummer kept the beat behind him. Another musician played bass guitar. They didn't have a backup singer. The band was just the three men.

Jim stepped forward to the microphone and sang a love song he had written. The song was one of the old tunes he and I had performed all those years ago.

When I pushed through the crowd to the stage, he looked down at me as he sang. But I could tell he didn't recognize me. Even back in the old days, he would often sing a song to one woman in the audience. This time he picked me.

All the same, the hair on my arms stood up. I felt as if I had made him appear, created him with my thoughts. Or as if the Coyote spirit had.

I stood there in front of the stage for three more songs. Then Jim announced that the band would take a short break. I waited by the stage while the crowd left.

Jim took the stairs down from the stage and headed towards me. He was probably on his way to grab some lunch at one of the hamburger stands. I could tell he still didn't recognize me, not at first. I almost let him pass by without saying hello.

But then he smiled at me as he went by.

"Jim," I said. "Is that really you?"

He turned and paused. "Sara?"

Neither of us knew what to say for a moment. Then he said, "Look what time has done to us."

That hurt. I was feeling middle-aged. I had put on a little weight during my pregnancy with Rose.

I never lost those pounds. And I had just found my first few grey hairs.

I knew I didn't look like the young woman Jim once knew. Time had changed me. That was why I almost let him walk by.

Then I realized that Jim might feel the same way. He, too, had gained a little weight, and his face had softened with middle age. He wasn't the young guy I had seen on my camera screen back at the children's stage.

But until the moment he spoke to me, I hadn't noticed he had grown older. While he played guitar and sang on stage, he was that young Jim. He was the musician I had known fifteen years before. I felt as if no time had passed at all.

"I heard your music on the radio," I said. "And I saw you on TV once, talking about a new CD."

"That must have been some time ago," he said. "I haven't released any new tunes for a while."

He grinned at me and took my hand. When he did that, I felt all my old feelings for him flood back. "Gosh, it's good to see you again," he said.

I looked down at Jim's hand holding mine. Jim's hand was warm and soft, so unlike my husband's rough hands. I noticed Jim wasn't wearing a wedding ring.

"It's good to see you, too," I said. I tried to make my voice sound calm. I tried to hold in the excitement I felt at seeing Jim again. I was, after all, a married woman.

"So, what have you been up to?" he asked. "Are you still singing? You were always writing songs when we were on the road. But then you would never show them to me."

"I didn't want you to see them," I said. "I knew they weren't all that great." I hesitated before telling him the truth of the matter. "I wanted to impress you," I said. "I had a crush on you."

In fact, I now knew that I had loved him back then. Then I realized that maybe I still did.

Chapter Four

Jim still had the rugged good looks that set the men of the Cowichan Tribes apart. The Cowichan Tribes is the name of a First Nations band on Vancouver Island. Jim grew up on the island, in Duncan, which calls itself the "City of Totems." Last I heard, he had returned there.

"You still on Vancouver Island?" I asked him.

"Only when I'm not touring with the band," he said. "These days I don't get home much."

"That's good news, right?" I asked. "Your band must be doing well."

"We play bars and clubs mostly," he said. "This gig, this job at the Roots and Blues Festival, is a big one for us. How about you? Where are you living?"

"On the Lightning Bay Reserve. You remember Jenny Moses?"

"Sure."

"We're in her old place." I glanced at the children's area. "Were you over at Fred Penner's stage just a few minutes ago?" I asked him. "I saw you there, in the children's area. I tried to catch up to you, but I couldn't find you."

Jim shook his head. "You must have seen someone else. I've been on stage with my band for the last hour or so."

"Now I *know* Coyote is playing tricks on me," I said. The Coyote spirit had shown me Jim was there, and then led me to him.

"What was that?" Jim asked me.

"Nothing," I said. I laughed. "I just feel so strange running into you here."

"Hey," Jim said. "Why don't you join us on stage after the break, for old time's sake? We sing a lot of the old songs."

"Oh, I don't think so," I said. "I'm not dressed for getting up on stage."

I looked down at myself. I had dressed up a little for our day at the festival, but these weren't stage clothes. I wore a pretty cotton skirt and a T-shirt.

I noticed my sandals were dusty from the festival grounds. I was glad I had at least painted my toenails that morning.

"You look great!" Jim said. "Beautiful, in fact." He grinned at me. From the way he looked at me, I knew he was telling the truth. He did find me beautiful. All at once I felt like my young self again.

But I shook my head. "I haven't sung on stage for years," I said.

"You remember the old songs, right?" Jim asked.

"Sure, I do." I sang them all the time in the shower. But I hadn't been in front of an audience for a long time. My daughter and my husband were the only ones who heard me sing now.

"Come on," said Jim. "You know you want to."

I did want to. The idea of singing on stage again with Jim thrilled me.

"I have to run it by my husband," I said. "He'll have to take care of our daughter. I'm not sure how he's going to feel about that. We don't get a lot of days together as a family. Rob must be wondering where the hell I've got to by now."

"So you're married?" Jim looked disappointed.

"And we've got a daughter named Rose," I said. "Did you ever get married?"

"No," he said. "But I'm tired of living alone. I'd like to find someone."

I looked into his face a moment. "I'm sure you will find someone," I said.

"It's hard to keep a romance going when you're on the road," Jim said.

I knew he was right. Shortly after I married Rob, I gave up touring. I no longer took singing jobs in other towns. I quit because Rob and I fought every time I came back from a gig away from home.

Rob wasn't jealous of other guys I might meet on the road. He trusted me. He just wanted me home. So I only took local gigs where I could come back to the house every night. I gave up singing altogether when I got pregnant with Rose.

"I'll go let Rob know what I'm up to," I said.

"Meet me back at the stage?"

I nodded. This was too good a chance to pass up. I was going to sing at the Roots and Blues Festival! But I knew I was in for a fight with my husband over it.

Chapter Five

I was right. I caught up with Rob and Rose back at the children's area. When I told my husband that I wanted to sing with Jim's band, he hated the idea.

"But we never get to spend a day together as a family," Rob said. "You've been complaining about that for months. Now you want to take off on us?"

During his work week, my husband and I hardly saw each other. Rob worked as a faller for a logging crew. He spent his days running a chainsaw, cutting down trees. The work was dangerous. A tree had fallen on his buddy and broken the man's back.

The work also wore Rob out. These August days, he headed into the bush at three o'clock in the morning to avoid the afternoon heat. He came home around one o'clock in the afternoon and took a nap. But he was so tired that he often slept into the evening.

"I'll only be on stage with Jim for an hour or two," I said.

Rob shook his head. "Let me get this straight. You want me to babysit Rose while you go off to sing with some old boyfriend."

"Jim was never my boyfriend."

"But you liked the guy, right?" Rob said. "I can tell."

"That was a long time ago," I said.

I glanced down at my daughter. Rob had bought Rose a hot dog and an apple juice while he waited for me. Rose sucked the straw on her juice box as she looked up at us.

"I don't want to argue in front of Rose," I said.

Music drifted towards us from several stages. I could hear Jim's voice singing. His band had already started up after their break. I would have to go now if I was going to sing with them.

"Listen, I've got to go," I said. "This means a lot to me."

I took my little girl's hand. "You see how much Rose loves to dance in front of people," I said. "That's me. There's a part of me that *must* get up on stage and sing. I haven't been able to do that for a long time."

"I thought you liked being a stay-at-home mom," Rob said.

"I do. But Rose starts school this fall. You're at work. I'm at home all alone. I need to do something for myself."

My husband looked off at the hundreds of people moving around the festival grounds. A stilt-walker towered over the crowd in the children's area. The man, walking on wooden poles tied to his legs, was dressed like a robot.

My daughter could not take her eyes off the stilt-walker. I lifted her up to give her a better view. But I couldn't hold Rose for long. She was getting so big. My little girl was growing so fast.

I put Rose down. "Why don't you come over and watch me sing?" I asked my husband. "Rose has never seen me on stage. She'll love it!"

Rose clapped her hands. "Can I sing with you?" she asked.

"Not this time," I said. "But I bet you'll be on stage sometime soon."

Rob nodded. "All right," he said. But he still didn't look too happy.

My family walked with me to the stage where Jim and his band performed. As soon as Jim saw us, he ended the song and introduced me. I went to the stage to sing the country love songs we had sung together fifteen years before.

Up there, in front of that audience, I felt like I had gone back in time. Jim and I were young and on tour. And Jim wasn't singing to some woman in the crowd. He was singing his love songs to me.

Then I glanced down into the audience. My daughter danced to the music. My husband was watching us, of course. When the song ended, Rose clapped for me with the rest of the crowd. But my husband didn't. He took our daughter by the hand and led her away.

Chapter Six

I sang a few more of the old songs with Jim. Then his band's time on stage ended. Jim walked me down the stage stairs.

"Where did your family go?" he asked me.

"I'm not sure," I said.

"I wanted to meet them, especially your little girl," Jim said. "I could tell, right away, that she was your daughter. She looks so much like you."

"She acts like me, too," I said. "She loves to dance and sing. She wanted to come up on stage to sing with us."

"She's a performer, all right," Jim said. "Just like her mom."

"Well, I'm not a singer anymore," I said. "That time of my life is over."

Jim took both my hands in his. "I don't believe that. Do you?"

Jim was so good-looking. His smile took my breath away.

I looked down at our hands and shrugged. I felt so happy and alive singing on stage with Jim. But I was a mom now. I couldn't live that life anymore.

"I should go," I said. "I told Rob and Rose I would meet them at the van if we got separated."

"I'll walk you to the parking lot, then," Jim said. "I want to meet them."

After the way Rob behaved, I didn't want my husband and Jim to meet. Rob was clearly jealous of Jim. Or maybe he was jealous of me singing on stage. But I couldn't convince Jim to stay with his band. He walked me across the festival grounds to the van.

Rob and Rose waited for me beside the van. My husband looked tired and angry. Rose sweated in the summer heat. I felt bad for making them wait while I sang.

Jim held out his hand to my husband and introduced himself. To my surprise, Rob shook his hand. Then Jim turned to my daughter and shook her hand.

"Are you famous?" Rose asked him.

"Sometimes," Jim said, "in some places." He winked at me.

"Jim is very well known," I said. "He won several music awards."

"But that was a while ago," Jim said.

"Did you win an award?" Rose asked me.

"No, honey," I said. "I was just a backup singer."

"Your mom is being modest," Jim said. "She made my music great. Things haven't been the same since she left the band."

"We should get going," Rob said. "It's been a long day for Rose."

"Yeah, and I should head back to the hotel for a nap," Jim said. "I've got another show tonight."

"It was good to meet you," Rob said to Jim.

"Same here," said Jim.

Jim handed me his business card. "Let's keep in touch," he said. "My e-mail address is on this card. I travel with my laptop computer and check my e-mail messages every day. Send me a message so I have your e-mail address, too."

"I will."

Then came that moment I'll never forget. My husband helped Rose into her car seat and got in the driver's seat. But, to be honest, I felt as if my family wasn't there. For that moment it was just Jim and I in that parking lot, looking at each other.

Jim hugged me and said, "Love you."

I knew what he meant, or at least I thought I did. He was glad that we had met again. The love he spoke of was the love of one old friend for another. But I was still a little shocked. I felt scared.

Even so, as he hugged me, I said, "Love you, too."

Then I glanced at Rob. He watched Jim and me through the open window of the van. Had he heard us?

I watched Jim as he walked across the parking lot. He waved once before disappearing into the crowd.

I wasn't sure I would ever see Jim again. I thought this was the end of it. But, as things turned out, it was only the beginning.

Chapter Seven

When we got home, I sat down at my computer and sent Jim an e-mail. The message was innocent enough, I thought. I told him how much I enjoyed seeing him again. I said I missed the days when we toured together with the band.

I sent the message and sat back in my chair, thinking of those days. But then, even before I got up from the computer to make supper, I received this reply:

Hello, Sara.

Wow. Singing with you again really brought back memories for me, too. There's something I wish I had told you many years ago. You said you had a crush on me back then. Well, I was in love with you. I just wasn't brave enough to say that to you. Imagine how different things would be if I had told you!

Jim

I read Jim's message again and again. I felt excited, and my cheeks grew warm. Jim had been in love with me! If Jim had told me he loved me all those years ago, would I still be touring with him today?

But then I would not have married Rob, and we wouldn't have had our daughter.

Rose laughed as she watched a television program in the living room. I was suddenly aware of my husband moving around behind me in the kitchen.

My husband and I shared our e-mail address. Rob would eventually see Jim's message if I left it on the computer. I would have to delete it. But I wanted to read Jim's message again and enjoy it a little. Jim had been in love with me!

So I left the message in our inbox, for the time being. I planned to delete it later, and anyway, Rob almost never checked our e-mail. I got up from the computer to make supper for my family.

"Is something wrong?" Rob asked me.

"No, I'm fine," I said.

"You look scared or something."

"I'm just tired," I said. "Performing on stage really wears me out."

That wasn't the truth, of course. I felt full of energy after singing with Jim. I felt alive!

As I made spaghetti, I thought about how great I felt on the stage earlier that day. I remembered how wonderful I felt around Jim. I was young and beautiful. I was myself again.

"You're awfully quiet tonight," Rob said as we ate.

"Just thinking," I said.

"You're thinking about *him*," Rob said. I knew he meant Jim.

I glanced at Rose. Her attention seemed to be on her noodles. "Please don't start," I said. "I don't want to argue in front of Rose."

After dinner, Rob got Rose ready for bed. Then, he read a book to her, as he always did on Saturday nights. He didn't have the energy to do that on week nights. While he took care of Rose, I slipped back into the kitchen. I sat at the computer and sent Jim a message:

Hello, Jim.

What I really wanted to say in my last e-mail is how much I enjoyed your company. The older I get the more I realize how rare it is to find someone I really get along with. When I find a person like that, as I did today, I don't take it for granted. I get the idea that you feel the same way. So let's stay in each other's lives, okay?

   Sara

There, I thought. I said that I wanted to see Jim again. But I didn't come right out and say that I had been in love with him, too. I just said how much I enjoyed his friendship.

Then why did I feel so guilty and scared when I pressed Send?

I knew I shouldn't see Jim again. I knew my seeing him would upset Rob. But I *wanted* to see my friend again. I wanted to feel young and beautiful.

I just had no idea that would happen so soon.

Chapter Eight

That night, Rob and I sat in the living room, watching the eleven o'clock news. Then we heard a howl. We thought the cry came from a real coyote at first. Then we realized the sound came from a man, howling and yipping like a coyote. And he was right outside our house.

"What the hell?" Rob said.

He went to the window and I followed. There stood my old friend Jim, dressed in the cowboy outfit he wore on stage. With his face to the sky, he howled like a coyote again.

Jim's pickup truck, a brand new Dodge Ram, was parked behind him. So Jim makes enough money to drive a new vehicle, I thought. He must be doing well.

I opened the kitchen door. "What are you doing here?" I called to Jim.

Then I closed the door behind me. I didn't want my husband out there. I was afraid of what Rob might say to Jim.

Jim howled again, in answer to my question. Then he pointed at the full moon. The moon was red. I had forgotten that there would be a lunar eclipse that night. The Earth's shadow covering the moon made it look red.

"Doesn't it just make you want to howl?" Jim asked me.

"If I was a coyote, maybe," I said.

Jim yipped and howled again. A dog from down the street started howling with him.

"I got your e-mail," I said.

"And I got yours," he said. "Come on, howl!"

I laughed and glanced back at the living room window. My husband watched us from there. His arms were crossed. He looked angry.

"Howl!" Jim demanded. He howled again himself.

The moon was so red and lovely. Having my old friend there made me feel like my old self, when I wasn't afraid to try something new. So I joined him. I howled at the full moon, this strange red moon.

"Come sing with me at the Roots and Blues Festival again tomorrow," he said. "We have a show in the morning. It's Sunday, so maybe Rob can look after Rose so you can get away?"

I looked back at my husband watching from the window. I knew Rob wouldn't want me to sing again with Jim, especially after Jim's crazy howling. I would be in for another argument with my husband. But how could I pass up this chance to sing?

"Yes," I said. "Of course I'll sing with you."

Jim howled again, to celebrate. I joined him.

As we howled together at the moon, a thrill ran through me. I could step out of my little life for one more day. I could sing on stage again, as I had in the old days with Jim.

Then Rob opened the kitchen door. "What the hell are you doing?" he demanded.

I pointed up at the moon. "It's a lunar eclipse," I said. "The Earth's shadow is covering the moon."

"So you howl?"

Howling had seemed like the right thing to do at the time.

"I'm sorry," Jim said. "Howling was my idea. I guess it's pretty annoying."

"Why are you here?" Rob asked Jim.

Jim glanced at me.

"He wanted to show me the eclipse," I said. "There's no need to be rude."

"Do you know what time it is?" Rob asked.

"We just finished our show," said Jim. "It takes a while to pack up our gear after that. Then there was the drive out here."

"Jim came to ask if I would sing with the band tomorrow morning," I told Rob. "I said I would."

My husband pointed a finger at Jim. "You stay away from my wife."

"Rob!" I said.

I turned to Jim. "I'm so sorry."

"It's okay," Jim said. He glanced at Rob, and then turned back to me. "See you at the festival tomorrow?"

"I'll be there," I said.

Chapter Nine

Rob went inside as I watched Jim drive away in his pickup. A coyote trotted across the gravel road just after he left. I saw the glow of its eyes as it looked at me.

Maybe this was just an ordinary coyote. Or maybe it was the Coyote spirit from my Granny's stories.

In the old stories, Coyote was a hero for my people. This spirit brought us so many good things. But Coyote also loved to stir up trouble. And my old friend Jim was certainly trouble.

I took one last look at the red moon. Then I took a deep breath and went inside. I knew I was about to have another fight with Rob.

The TV and all the lights in the house were off. I felt my way to the bedroom through the dark. But

Rob had shut the door. So there I stood, knocking on my very own bedroom door.

"What?" Rob said.

I went into the room and sat on the bed next to my husband. The room smelled like him, like the pine trees he cut down each work day. There wasn't enough light from the red moon to see him properly. All I saw was the dark outline of his face against the window.

"What the hell was that about?" I asked him.

"You were flirting with Jim," Rob said. "You were howling at the moon with him, for god's sake. I can tell you like him."

"Of course I like him," I said. "He's an old friend. I haven't seen him for a long time. I enjoy his company."

"No, you're attracted to him."

"It's not like that," I said.

"No? Are you sure?"

"You really should have stopped to take a look at the moon," I said. I was trying to change the subject. "I've hardly ever seen the moon turn red like that. You could see the Earth's shadow on it."

"You didn't want me out there with you and Jim," Rob said.

"What do you mean?"

"You blushed when you talked to Jim this afternoon," he said. "You played with your hair. You only have eyes for him when you're together. When you stood by the van today at the festival, neither of you even knew I was there."

I felt embarrassed. My husband had noticed everything I felt when I was with Jim. I had hidden nothing.

"I'm sorry," I said. "Seeing Jim again is a big deal for me. He's a dear friend. I love singing and he's given me the chance to be on stage again."

"But it's not just that, is it?" Rob said. "You feel different. Even since you ran into Jim today, you've acted different. I feel like I don't even know you. Look at you, howling at the moon like a coyote."

Rob was right. I did feel different. Everything was different. I felt like my old self again.

I patted my chest. "This *is* me. What you saw tonight is the part of myself I can never let out here, at home."

"Jim lets your coyote out. He makes you howl."

I laughed. "I guess," I said.

"I don't want you to see him again."

"I *am* singing with Jim in the band's show tomorrow morning," I said.

"No, you're not."

"It's a huge opportunity for me," I said. "Singing on stage with him tomorrow could restart my career."

"What career? You can't make a living singing."

"Jim does," I said.

"He's on the road all the time," said Rob. "He's never home. You told me so yourself."

"I'm not going to miss this opportunity to sing at the Roots and Blues Festival," I said.

"Is your singing really worth more than our marriage?" asked Rob.

"I shouldn't have to choose one over the other."

"It seems that you do," he said.

"Don't make me choose," I said. "Don't lose me."

Chapter Ten

After our show at the festival the next morning, Jim took me for lunch. We went to one of the many burger stands on the festival grounds. I sat at a picnic table while he bought the burgers, fries, and Cokes.

Jim had dressed for the stage as he had in the old days. He wore jeans, a western shirt, cowboy boots, and a cowboy hat. I admit I noticed how nicely his jeans fit his behind. I looked away quickly when he turned around with our lunch.

"Your husband didn't seem too pleased to see me last night," Jim said. He sat my burger down in front of me. "Should you be here with me?"

I blushed. "We did have a fight last night," I said. "But this is important to me. I haven't been on stage for a long time."

Jim took a drink of his Coke. "Rob is jealous of me."

"I'm not really sure if he's jealous of you or my singing."

"Why would he be jealous of your singing?"

"He likes me at home," I said. "He doesn't want me to work."

"He can't expect you to give up your career for him."

"That's what I told him," I said. "Anyway, he shouldn't be jealous of you. Every woman needs friends, other than her husband."

"Is that what we are? Friends?"

"Of course," I said.

Jim looked disappointed. "But you feel a special connection with me. You said as much in your e-mail."

"Yes," I said. "It's a rare thing to feel that with someone."

"What do you suppose that's about?" Jim asked me. He grinned.

"You tell me what you think it's about," I said.

"You first."

I didn't say anything. I felt my face grow hot. I started to panic.

"I should go," I said.

"You haven't finished your burger."

"I can't expect Rob to take care of Rose all day," I said. "Today is his day off. He has things he wants to do. He has to work all week."

"Yes, of course."

Jim walked me back to the van. He hugged me goodbye. I found myself holding on to him a little too long. I didn't want to let go.

"How about a kiss?" he said. He gave me a brief, friendly peck on the lips. Then he said, "I really was in love with you, you know."

"I was in love with you, too," I said.

"I guess that was a long time ago."

"Yes," I said.

As Jim walked away, I called to him, "Tell me why you think we get along so well."

"You tell me first," he said. Then he waved goodbye.

When I got home, Rose was playing in her room. Rob lay on the couch with his eyes closed. He didn't say hello.

"Thanks for watching Rose while I did the show," I said.

But Rob ignored me, as if I wasn't there.

That hurt. I had my first real chance to sing in years, and my husband didn't even ask how it went. I felt mad that Rob wasn't happy for me. Jim helped me, he felt proud of my singing, but not Rob. What was I doing in this marriage?

I stomped out of the living room. I sat down at the computer in the kitchen and started an e-mail message to Jim.

"Why do we get along so well?" I wrote to him. "Here's what I think. You said you were in love with me all those years ago. I was in love with you, too. I think maybe I still am."

Then I hit the Send button. I sat back. In moments Jim would know how I felt. And my marriage would almost certainly come to an end.

Chapter Eleven

After I sent that e-mail to Jim, I went to check on my daughter. Rose was dancing in her room to the music in a wind-up music box. She was so beautiful.

I couldn't take Rose with me if I went on tour with Jim and his band. How would she go to school? But I couldn't leave her at home, either.

I felt cold from panic. What had I done? I would have to delete the messages between Jim and me before Rob saw them.

But when I left Rose's room, Rob was at the computer. Our inbox was open on the screen in front of him. He had found the e-mail exchange between Jim and me.

"I knew you e-mailed Jim when you got home," Rob said. "I just knew it. You should have deleted the messages right away."

I felt sick to my stomach. "Oh, Rob," I said. "I'm so sorry."

"There's one here from Jim that I don't think you've seen yet," he said.

I looked at the screen. There I saw Jim's reply: "So you love me, eh? Well, in case you didn't notice, I love you, too. I've always loved you."

I turned away. I felt dizzy. My husband had seen everything.

"Have you slept with him already?" Rob asked me. "When did you have time? You only ran into him yesterday, for god's sake. Or did you see him before?"

"No," I said. "We haven't even kissed."

Well, not really, I thought. Jim's kiss was only a peck, a friendly kiss. At least that's what I had thought at the time. I realized now that when Jim kissed me, he was trying to tell me how he felt.

"Then what is all this about?" Rob asked.

I hesitated. "I'm not sure," I said. "Jim makes me feel brave, like I could do anything I set my mind to."

"And I don't."

"You tried to stop me from singing at the festival," I said.

"No, I tried to stop you from seeing this guy." Rob pointed at Jim's message on the computer screen. "*Are* you in love with him?"

With Jim I was a singer, a performer. With Rob I was a wife and mother, a housekeeper. Jim excited me. But did that mean I loved him? I wasn't sure now.

"I'm sorry," I said. "I honestly don't know what this is all about. All I know is that Jim makes me feel like myself again. I love singing. I love getting up on stage."

"And I stand in your way."

"No." I waved my hand, trying to make sense of my own thoughts.

I started again. "We just got so busy," I said. "When Rose was born there wasn't much time for anything but taking care of her and keeping house. I feel guilty when I do anything for myself. You made it clear you didn't want me to sing anymore."

"I was tired," Rob said. "I wanted to rest when I got home. I didn't have the energy to work and then take care of Rose while you went out to sing in the evening. And I wanted to spend the evenings with you."

"I get tired, too," I said. "I spend all day being a mom and taking care of the house. That's real work, too. You rest when you come home. But my day doesn't end."

Rob nodded slowly. He understood. "I've been a jerk, haven't I?" he said.

"No, I've been the jerk," I said. I pointed at the computer screen, at the place in the message where Jim said he loved me, too.

"So what do we do now?" Rob asked me.

"I don't know."

"Are you going to leave me?" Rob asked. "Will you go off with this guy? *Do* you love him?"

I loved the life I had once, with Jim. I loved singing on stage. I even enjoyed touring, driving from town to town to put on shows. I could have that life again with Jim.

"I don't know," I said again.

Chapter Twelve

When I saw Jim drive into our yard, I stepped outside. I closed the kitchen door behind me. I didn't want another argument with Rob, not now.

My husband was asleep in his La-Z-Boy chair in the living room. He often slept on Sunday afternoons. He never got enough sleep during the week. And now he was even more tired out from our arguments.

Rose was in the kitchen making little masks out of play dough. The masks Rose made were like the traditional masks Rob once carved out of wood. My husband had been a real artist. But he didn't have time for that now.

Neither my husband nor my daughter could see Jim and me from where they were. They would have to stand at a window to see us.

Jim wore jeans and a T-shirt. I knew he would soon have to get dressed for his evening show. He should have been at the festival already, setting up his gear on stage.

"Don't you have a show tonight?" I asked. "What are you doing here?"

"I tried phoning but there was no answer," Jim said as he walked up to the door. "You didn't answer my e-mails. Our last show starts in less than two hours and I want you up on stage with me."

"Rob saw our e-mails," I said. "I unplugged the phone while we tried to work things out."

"Shit."

"He has every right to be angry," I said.

"Have you told him what you're going to do?"

"I don't know what to tell him yet."

Jim took my hands. "Tell him you have a man who loves you. Tell him you're going to sing with me and the band. We'll go on the road together."

"With my daughter?"

"I imagine Rose would stay here with her dad, at least during the school year."

I pulled my hands away. "I could never leave her."

"So, we'll take Rose too," he said. "We'll work something out. You said your daughter was born for the stage. She will love that life as much as you do."

"I need some time," I said. "I've got to think this through."

"I understand," said Jim. "But sing with me tonight. This is our last show of the festival. I want you there."

I looked back at the house to make sure no one was watching from the window. There, in the living room, was the furniture Rob and I picked out together. I saw the back of the La-Z-Boy chair where Rob was sleeping right now. There were our family photos on the side tables. Many of the masks Rob had carved hung on the walls.

Everything in that room reminded me of our family's happy life together. I didn't really know I was missing anything until Coyote, and Jim, turned up.

Now I knew I *had* to sing. Jim offered me that opportunity, and more.

"Can you do something for me?" I asked Jim.

"Sure," he said. "Anything."

"Kiss me," I said.

Jim glanced at the house. He laughed. "Okay." He gave me a peck on the lips, like the kiss he had given me yesterday. A friendly kiss.

"No," I said. "*Kiss* me. Like you mean it."

He grinned. "With pleasure!"

He took me in his arms and kissed me full on the mouth. The kiss was passionate. This was the kind of kiss Rob had given me when we first fell in love. My husband hadn't kissed me like that for a long time. I had dreamed of kissing Jim like that when I first knew him many years before.

But something was missing. The kiss wasn't right. Not here. Not in my family's yard. Not with everything that Rob and I had worked so hard to build all around me.

"Are you going to sing with me tonight?" Jim asked.

I rubbed my forehead. "I don't know," I said.

Jim looked at his watch. "You'll have to decide soon," he said. "You know where to find me."

Chapter Thirteen

Jim got in his truck and I went back inside. I watched through the kitchen window as he drove away, and Rose stood with me. My daughter smelled of the strawberry shampoo I'd washed her hair with.

"Is that guy your boyfriend?" she asked me.

A chill ran through me. My little girl had seen Jim kiss me.

"No," I said.

"He's your friend?" Rose asked.

I knew my daughter was trying to work things out. She was trying to figure out what this man Jim meant to me and my family. I was trying to figure that out, too.

I thought for a moment about Jim. He made me feel beautiful and desired. He made me feel strong, like I could do anything. He made me want to sing again. I felt alive, now, in a way I hadn't in years.

"He's my hero," I said finally.

"Daddy's *my* hero," Rose said.

I looked over at Rob asleep in his La-Z-Boy chair in the living room. His face showed how worn out he was. He looked tired even in his sleep.

Rose was right. Rob was a hero. He went to work every morning before I woke, so I could stay home and be with our daughter. His work cutting down trees was dangerous. Rob risked his life every day for us.

I went over to my husband. Rob turned a bit in his sleep. Now the sun coming through the window lit part of his face. I saw the lines that had begun to form in the corners of his eyes. I could imagine what he would look like as an elder. When I married him I had been so sure we would grow old together.

Now I wasn't so sure. I wasn't sure at all.

I woke him. "Rob?" I said.

"What?" He was still half asleep.

"Don't you ever want more than this?" I asked my husband. "More than working and taking care of the house?"

"Sure I do," Rob said. He sat up. "You think I like getting up to cut trees at three o'clock every morning? I was an artist once, remember? I used to be a carver. I stopped all that so I could make a living for you and Rose."

Rob carved traditional masks, just as his great-grandfather had. Once, some of his masks had even been chosen for a big First Nations art show. For several weeks, the masks had hung on the walls of the Kamloops Art Gallery.

I felt stupid then. I had given up my singing. But Rob had given up his carving, too. I knew he loved to carve as much as I loved to sing.

I also knew I was being selfish. But I couldn't go back to the way things were. I wanted to sing. I wanted to feel the way Jim made me feel.

"Can you watch Rose?" I asked my husband. "I have to go."

"Where?" he asked.

"I've just got to go."

I gave Rose a hug and got in the van. I wasn't sure where I was going. I just needed to think. Driving helped clear my mind.

The lake, the blue hills around me, everything felt new. This was the gift Jim gave me. He woke me up. I was myself again. But did that mean I loved him? If I did, did I love him enough to give up my marriage?

I came to an intersection. The light was red, so I stopped. I could continue straight and go to the festival, to Jim. He and the band would start their last show of the festival in less than an hour.

Or I could turn right and head back towards home and my husband.

I squeezed the steering wheel, trying to make up my mind. Then I noticed my wedding ring reflecting the sunlight. As I waited for the light to change, I pulled the ring off my finger. After sitting there all those years, the ring had left its mark, a band of silky skin.

Everything clicked for me then. I knew what I had to do. I slipped the ring back on my finger. When the light turned green, I went straight, to the festival.

Chapter Fourteen

The festival was beautiful in the evening light. The many stages were lit up. The sunset gave everything a red glow. The crowd was a flutter of colour. I felt the excitement I always felt before getting up to sing in front of people.

Jim was already on stage playing with his band when I arrived. Jim and the other members of the band were dressed in their cowboy outfits. I was only dressed in jeans and a T-shirt. I felt shy, for a moment, about getting up on stage with them.

Jim sang one of my favourite old tunes, a love song he had written. When Jim saw me standing in the crowd, he waved me up. I felt my heart begin to beat faster.

I joined Jim on stage and took my place at the microphone. Jim sang right to me, and I sang right back to him. The song we sang was about losing love, the end of an affair. We both belted out the last words as the song ended: "And I'll miss you."

Jim and I stepped back from the microphone as the crowd clapped and cheered.

"Glad you could join us," Jim said to me.

"I had to come," I said. "I couldn't miss this chance to sing with you again."

Then Jim stepped back to the microphone and introduced me. "Give Sara a big hand," he said. The crowd clapped again as I gave a little bow.

I felt so good on that stage. This was where I wanted to be. I knew it.

Across the field of the festival, lights twinkled as the evening sun faded. Jim and I sang and sang. The crowd at our feet danced, many waving their hands in the air. I felt as if I had never left this stage, as if I had always been here. I belonged here.

The stars began to come out. The moon rose. For a time, I saw the coyote sitting in the crowd below.

When I pointed at the coyote as we sang, Jim didn't seem to see it. But then, halfway through a song, Jim turned to the moon and howled like a coyote. The audience howled with him, and I howled, too. Jim grinned at me.

At the end of the song, Jim stepped back from the microphone and whispered in my ear. "I love you," he said.

I didn't respond. I just nodded, and we moved on to the next song. He glanced at me just once during that song. He was hurt that I didn't say, I love you, too.

Our show ended and the crowd broke up. The other members of the band started packing the equipment. Jim and the rest of the band would head out in the morning. They would go to their next gig, a festival in Alberta.

"I want you to come," Jim said. "I know you said you needed time. But we're so good together. We're meant to be on stage together. You know we are."

"I love singing with you," I said. "But when we're not on stage?" I shook my head. "I have a family. I can't pick up and leave."

"I don't understand," Jim said. "You said you love me."

"I love how you make me feel," I said. "I love that you believe in me. I love how we sing together. But all that is on stage. That's not real life."

"All that could be real life," Jim said. "That can be our life."

"I already have a life," I said. "I have a daughter. I have a husband. I have a home."

"You could have all that with me," Jim said.

I shook my head again. "I'm not going with you. I won't join the band."

"I don't believe you," Jim said. "You can't give this up."

"I already did," I said. "I gave up this life many years ago. I'm sorry, Jim."

I started to walk away. But then Jim howled at the moon.

I turned back and kissed Jim's cheek. "Thank you," I said. "For everything."

I walked through the crowd and left the festival grounds. I didn't look back.

Chapter Fifteen

When I got home the light of the moon lit up the yard. But the moon was no longer red. A lunar eclipse lasts only a few hours, not forever. This night's moon was the same old moon I had always known.

Rose was already asleep. Her room was dark. From outside the house, I saw Rob sitting alone on the couch in the living room, watching TV.

A coyote trotted across the field behind our house just then. It stopped when it reached our lawn. I could see its eyes shining in the moonlight. Was it the Coyote spirit, or just an ordinary wild animal?

A train clacked down the track in the distance, over at Notch Hill. When the train horn sounded at a crossing, the coyote on our lawn raised its long nose and howled. Some distance away, another coyote took up its song, yipping in the night.

I joined them, singing like a coyote. I knew that would get Rob's attention.

Rob got up to look out the living room window at me. Then he walked through the house and opened the kitchen door.

I thought my husband would scare the coyote away when he came outside. But the animal stayed where it was, watching us. I knew then that this was the Coyote spirit. This was the Coyote I had seen at the festival, the Coyote that had led me to Jim.

"What the hell are you doing?" Rob asked me.

"Just singing," I said, "with Coyote."

I pointed out Coyote, watching us from the long grasses where our lawn met the edge of the field. But my husband couldn't see him.

"Have you gone crazy?" Rob said.

"A little, I think," I said. "I did go crazy this weekend. But that was Coyote's fault."

Rob didn't laugh. He was still mad at me. But, of course, he would be.

"Rose was worried," Rob said. "I told her you were singing at the festival."

I nodded. "I was. I sang with Jim and the band during their last show."

"So you've made up your mind," Rob said.

"Yes, I have."

I walked up to my husband at the kitchen door and kissed him. I kissed him like I had when we were first in love. Rob resisted at first, but then he relaxed into the kiss. He kissed me back with that same passion we had felt years ago.

A feeling came over me that I knew well. This was how I used to feel when I was away on tour and about to return. I felt like I was on a familiar road, heading home. I belonged on stage. But I also belonged here with Rob and Rose.

"I love you," I said. "I love you and Rose more than anything. More than singing or being on stage."

"More than you love Jim?"

"I don't love Jim," I said. "I love how Jim made me feel. But I figured out that it isn't Jim that makes me feel that way. Doing what I love makes me feel that way."

"You want to sing again."

"Yes. But I don't need Jim for that. And I don't have to go on the road to do it. I don't want to be away from you and Rose even for one night. I'll find a way to sing here, around home. Okay?"

Rob nodded. "Okay," he said.

"And I want to help you find the time to carve again," I said. "Maybe if I make a bit of money with my singing gigs, you can cut back to a four-day work week."

"Maybe," he said. He grinned.

I kissed Rob again, and then *he* howled like a coyote. I howled, too. The coyote that had been watching us joined in for a few minutes. Our howls and yips echoed through the night sky. Then my husband took me by the hand and led me back into our home.

Good Reads

Discover Canada's Bestselling Authors with Good Reads Books

Good Reads authors have a special talent—
the ability to tell a great story, using clear language.

Good Reads can be purchased as eBooks, downloadable
direct to your mobile phone, eReader or computer.
Some titles are also available as audio books.

To find out more, please visit
www.GoodReadsBooks.com

The Good Reads project is sponsored by
ABC Life Literacy Canada.

Grass Roots Press

Good Reads Series

Tribb's Troubles

By Trevor Cole

Tribb has always been a thinker, not a doer. But he needs to do something about the mice in his house, and fast.

Linda, his wife, hates those mice. If only Tribb could get rid of the nasty little things. Then Linda might be happy again. Maybe even fall in love with him again.

Tribb has his troubles, all right. Mouse trouble. Marriage trouble. In the end, though, Tribb solves his problems. Or does he?

About the Author

By the age of eighteen, Gail Anderson-Dargatz knew that she wanted to write about Canadian women in rural settings. Today, Gail is a bestselling author. *A Recipe for Bees* and *The Cure for Death by Lightning* were finalists for the Giller prize. She currently teaches fiction in the creative writing program at the University of British Columbia. Gail divides her time between Manitoulin Island and the Shuswap region of BC, the landscape found in so much of her writing.

Also by Gail Anderson-Dargatz:

The Miss Hereford Stories
The Cure for Death by Lightning
A Recipe for Bees
A Rhinestone Button
Turtle Valley
The Stalker

You can visit Gail's website at
www.gailanderson-dargatz.ca